EVERYDAY CHOCOLATE

120 TASTY RECIPES

© 2010 by Barbour Publishing, Inc.

ISBN 978-1-60260-964-8

All rights reserved. No part of this publication may be reproduced or transmitted for commercial purposes, except for brief quotations in printed reviews, without written permission of the publisher.

All scripture quotations are taken from the King James Version of the Bible.

Published by Barbour Publishing, Inc., P.O. Box 719, Uhrichsville, Ohio 44683, www.barbourbooks.com

Our mission is to publish and distribute inspirational products offering exceptional value and biblical encouragement to the masses.

 Member of the
Evangelical Christian
Publishers Association

Printed in China.

INSPIRATION
at your fingertips!

If you're a lover of chocolate, this book is for you. Within these pages, you'll find dozens of indulgent recipes that are easy to prepare and are a delight to share with family and friends.

Finding a recipe is as easy as flipping through the book. Along the edge of each page, you'll see a color that corresponds to one of five categories:

So set this little book on your countertop, flip page after page for new culinary inspiration and kitchen tips and tricks, and you might just find a little encouragement in the process. Enjoy!

Candies & Other Treats

Delight thyself also in the LORD; and he shall give thee the desires of thine heart.
PSALM 37:4

LAYERED CHOCOLATE MINTS

¾ cup semisweet chocolate chips
¾ cup white chocolate chips
1 teaspoon peppermint extract
¾ cup milk chocolate chips

. . . .

In microwave-safe bowl, melt semisweet chocolate chips on high for 30-second intervals until melted. Pour into 8x8-inch pan lined with foil. Spread evenly. Allow to cool completely. Let stand until firm. In microwave-safe bowl, melt white chocolate chips on high for 30-second intervals or until melted. Stir in peppermint extract. Mix thoroughly. Pour white chocolate mixture over semisweet chocolate. Spread evenly. Allow to cool completely. Let stand until firm. In microwave-safe bowl, melt milk chocolate chips on high for 30-seconds intervals or until melted. Pour over white chocolate. Spread evenly. Refrigerate for at least 2 hours. Remove from pan. Cut into 2-inch squares.

CHOCOLATE TRUFFLES

½ cup unsalted butter, softened
2½ cups powdered sugar, plus extra for topping
½ cup cocoa
¼ cup heavy cream
1½ teaspoons vanilla

Center: Pecans, walnuts, almonds, or after-dinner mints
Coating: Flaked coconut, crushed nuts, or powdered sugar

....

In large bowl, cream butter. In separate bowl, combine powdered sugar and cocoa; add to butter alternately with cream and vanilla. Blend well. Chill until firm. Shape small amount of mixture around desired center; roll into 1-inch balls. Drop into desired coating and turn until well covered. Chill until firm.

EASY BLENDER MOUSSE

7 ounces dark chocolate
1/4 cup boiling water
1/2 cup heavy cream
1/2 teaspoon vanilla
1 egg

Break up chocolate into blender. Add boiling water. Blend for 30 seconds. Add remaining ingredients. Blend 15 seconds. Scrape down sides. Blend until smooth. Pour into dessert dishes or glasses and refrigerate 3 to 4 hours until set.

TURTLES

3 cups melting chocolate
1 cup coarsely chopped walnuts
½ cup chopped pecans
½ cup chopped almonds
½ teaspoon vanilla

....

Line cookie sheet with waxed paper. In medium saucepan over low heat, melt chocolate until smooth. Stir in walnuts, pecans, almonds, and vanilla. Remove from heat. Drop by teaspoons onto prepared sheet. Chill.

CHOCOLATE CARAMELS

2½ tablespoons butter
2 cups molasses
1 cup brown sugar
½ cup whole milk
1 square semisweet baking chocolate, chopped
1 teaspoon vanilla

. . . .

In saucepan, combine butter, molasses, brown sugar, and milk. Cook over low heat until butter is melted and mixture is blended well. Add chocolate. Stirring constantly, heat until chocolate is completely melted. Boil until candy thermometer reads 248 degrees. Remove from heat. Add vanilla. Blend completely. Pour into buttered 8x8-inch pan. Cut into squares.

CHOCOLATE PEANUT BUTTER CUPS

1 (12 ounce) package milk chocolate chips, divided
1 cup peanut butter
½ cup powdered sugar

. . . .

Trim 12 paper muffin cup liners to half their
height. In microwavable bowl, microwave half
the chocolate chips for 2 minutes, stirring after
each minute. Spoon melted chocolate into muffin
cups, filling halfway. With spoon, spread chocolate
up sides of cups until evenly coated. Cool in
refrigerator until firm. In small bowl, mix together
peanut butter and powdered sugar. Divide evenly
into chocolate cups. Melt remaining chocolate
and spoon over peanut butter mixture. Spread
chocolate to edges of cups.

REMARKABLE FUDGE

4 cups sugar
2 (5 ounce) cans evaporated milk
1 cup butter
1 (7 ounce) jar marshmallow crème
1 cup milk chocolate chips
1 teaspoon vanilla
1 cup chopped nuts (optional)
2 cups semisweet chocolate chips

....

Line 9x13-inch baking pan with foil, extending foil over edges of pan. Butter foil; set pan aside. Butter sides of large, heavy saucepan. Combine sugar, milk, and butter in saucepan. Cook and stir over medium-high heat until mixture boils. Reduce heat to medium; continue cooking for 10 minutes, stirring constantly. Remove pan from heat. Add remaining ingredients and stir until chocolate melts. Beat by hand for 1 minute. Spread in prepared pan. Score into 1-inch pieces while still warm. When fudge is firm, use foil to lift out of pan. Cut fudge into squares. Store in tightly covered container in refrigerator. Makes about 3 pounds.

HANDY CONVERSIONS

1 teaspoon = 5 milliliters
1 tablespoon = 15 milliliters
1 fluid ounce = 30 milliliters
1 cup = 250 milliliters
1 pint = 2 cups (or 16 fluid ounces)
1 quart = 4 cups (or 2 pints or
32 fluid ounces)
1 gallon = 16 cups (or 4 quarts)
1 peck = 8 quarts
1 bushel = 4 pecks
1 pound = 454 grams

Quick
Chart

Fahrenheit	Celsius
250°–300°	121°–149°
300°–325°	149°–163°
325°–350°	163°–177°
375°	191°
400°–425°	204°–218°

CHOCOLATE COVERED CHERRIES

2½ cups sugar
¼ cup margarine
1 tablespoon milk
½ teaspoon almond extract
4 (4 ounce) jars maraschino cherries with stems, drained
2 cups semisweet chocolate chips
2 tablespoons shortening

••

In medium bowl, combine sugar, margarine, milk, and almond extract; stir. On lightly floured surface, knead mixture into large ball. Roll into 1-inch balls. Flatten balls into 2-inch circles. Leaving stems sticking out, wrap cherries in circles by lightly rolling in hands. Place wrapped cherries on sheet of waxed paper and chill in refrigerator for at least 4 hours. In medium saucepan over medium heat, melt chocolate chips and shortening. Holding balls by stems of cherries sticking out, dip chilled balls into chocolate mixture. Chill in refrigerator.

MARSHMALLOW CUPS

2 cups milk chocolate chips
2 tablespoons shortening
1 cup marshmallow crème

Line mini muffin baking pans with 18 foil cups. In saucepan over low heat, melt chocolate chips with shortening, stirring constantly. Spoon ½ tablespoon chocolate mixture into each cup, using back of spoon to spread chocolate up sides of each cup. Spoon 1 tablespoon marshmallow crème into each cup. Spoon ½ tablespoon remaining chocolate over each marshmallow cup. Refrigerate until firm.

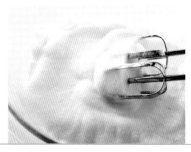

CHOCOLATE COFFEE BEANS

¼ cup dark roasted coffee beans, whole
½ cup milk chocolate chips

....

Break whole coffee beans in half along ridge
on bean. In small saucepan over low heat, melt
chocolate chips, stirring until smooth. Drop
coffee bean halves into chocolate by handfuls.
Stir beans into chocolate and scoop out with a
slotted spoon. Place on waxed paper-lined cookie
sheet to harden. Separate so they do not clump
together.

RASPBERRY TRUFFLES

2 cups semisweet chocolate chips
¾ cup sweetened condensed milk
¼ cup raspberry jam
2 tablespoons butter
½ cup white chocolate chips

In saucepan over low heat, melt semisweet chips, condensed milk, jam, and butter, stirring constantly. Pour into pie pan. Refrigerate until mixture is thick but soft, about 1½ hours. Form into 1-inch balls. Place on baking sheet lined with waxed paper. In microwavable bowl, melt white chocolate chips on high for 1 minute. Stir. Melt on high for 30 seconds more or until completely melted. Spoon melted chocolate over top of each truffle ball, allowing chocolate to drip slightly down sides of each ball. Refrigerate until chocolate is firm. Store in refrigerator.

BUCKEYES

2 cups butter
2 cups peanut butter
2½ pounds powdered sugar
3 teaspoons vanilla
melting chocolate

....

In large bowl, cream butter
and peanut butter. Add
powdered sugar and mix
well. Add vanilla and mix
well. Roll into balls the
size of large marbles. In
double boiler over low
heat, melt chocolate chips.
Use toothpick to dip balls
in chocolate about halfway.
Place on waxed paper to
cool.

WHITE CHOCOLATE TRUFFLES

1 (12 ounce) package white chocolate chips
⅓ cup whipping cream
2 teaspoons orange extract
1 teaspoon orange zest
1 cup powdered sugar

....

In saucepan over low heat, melt chocolate chips with cream, stirring constantly. Whisk in extract and zest until blended. Pour into pie pan. Refrigerate until mixture is thick but soft, about 2 hours. Shape mixture into 1-inch balls. Roll in powdered sugar. Place in small foil cups.

COCONUT ALMOND BARS

2 cups powdered sugar
1 cup flaked coconut
$\frac{1}{3}$ cup plus 1 tablespoon sweetened condensed
   milk
1 teaspoon vanilla
1 cup slivered almonds
$\frac{1}{2}$ cup milk chocolate chips
$\frac{1}{2}$ cup semisweet chocolate chips
1 tablespoon butter

....

Combine powdered sugar, coconut, condensed milk, vanilla, and almonds in medium bowl. Stir with wooden spoon until thoroughly blended. Press into buttered 8x8-inch pan. Melt chocolate chips with butter in small saucepan over low heat, stirring constantly. Spread evenly over coconut mixture in pan. Refrigerate until almost firm. Cut into bars. Store in refrigerator.

CHOCO-PEANUT BUTTER BARS

1 cup butter, softened
4 cups powdered sugar
1 cup crunchy peanut butter
1 cup graham cracker crumbs
1 (12 ounce) package semisweet chocolate chips

In mixing bowl, blend butter, powdered sugar, peanut butter, and crumbs. Press into buttered 9x13-inch baking pan. In microwavable bowl, melt chocolate chips on high for 1 minute. Stir. Heat for 30 seconds more or until completely melted. Spread evenly over peanut butter mixture. Chill until chocolate is firm.

NO SMUDGES

Wear a pair of latex or neoprene gloves when handling your chocolate-covered treats to avoid transferring fingerprints before they're served to guests or friends.

Quick Tip

MOCHA FUDGE

1 tablespoon instant coffee
1 tablespoon boiling water
2½ cups sugar
½ cup butter
1 (5 ounce) can evaporated milk
1½ cups semisweet chocolate chips
1 (7 ounce) jar marshmallow crème
½ teaspoon vanilla

....

Dissolve coffee in boiling water. Set aside. In saucepan, combine sugar, butter, and evaporated milk. Bring to a boil over medium heat, stirring constantly. Boil for 5 minutes. Remove from heat. Stir in coffee mixture, chocolate chips, marshmallow crème, and vanilla. Pour into buttered 9x9-inch pan. Let stand at room temperature for 1 hour. Cut into 1-inch squares. Cover. Refrigerate until fudge is set.

CHOCO-BUTTERSCOTCH CRISPS

1 cup butterscotch chips
½ cup peanut butter
4 cups crispy rice cereal
1 cup semisweet chocolate chips
2 tablespoons butter
1 tablespoon water
½ cup powdered sugar

....

Melt butterscotch chips and peanut butter over very low heat, stirring occasionally. Add cereal and mix well. Press half of mixture in 8x8-inch buttered baking pan and chill. Melt chocolate chips, butter, and water in top of double boiler and add powdered sugar. Spread over chilled mixture and press in remainder of cereal mixture. Cut and chill in refrigerator

WHITE CHOCOLATE PRETZELS

1 cup white chocolate chips
1 bag pretzel twists
Sprinkles (optional)

....

In double boiler over low heat, melt white
chocolate chips, stirring until smooth. Dip pretzels
in chocolate until completely coated. Remove
using pair of tongs. Place on waxed paper to cool.
Decorate with sprinkles if desired.

CHOCOLATE TOFFEE

1 cup butter
1 cup brown sugar
1 cup pecan pieces
1 (6 ounce) package milk chocolate chips

In saucepan, melt butter and brown sugar over low heat, stirring constantly. Let boil for 10 minutes, still stirring. Spread pecan pieces into greased 9x13-inch pan. Pour butter-brown sugar mixture over nuts. When set but still warm, sprinkle chocolate chips on top and allow to melt. When completely cooled, cut into 1-inch pieces.

ROCKY ROAD DELIGHTS

2 cups milk chocolate chips
¼ cup butter
1 teaspoon vanilla
1 cup mini marshmallows
2 cups chopped walnuts

....

In double boiler, slowly melt milk chocolate chips
and butter. Remove from heat. Stir in vanilla,
marshmallows, and nuts. Mix thoroughly. Pour into
buttered 8x8-inch pan. Refrigerate until firm.

COOKIE BARK

1 (20 ounce) package chocolate sandwich cookies, divided
2 (18½ ounce) packages white chocolate, divided

....

Line 10x15-inch jellyroll pan with waxed paper. Coat paper with nonstick cooking spray; set aside. Break half of cookies into coarse pieces and place in large bowl. In microwave-safe bowl, melt one package of white chocolate in microwave. Quickly fold melted chocolate into broken cookie pieces. Pour mixture into prepared pan and spread to cover half of pan. Repeat process with remaining chocolate and cookies. Refrigerate until solid. Remove from pan and carefully peel off waxed paper. Place bark on large cutting board and cut into pieces with a large knife. Store in airtight container.

DOUBLE PEANUT BUTTER CHOCOLATE FUDGE

½ cup light corn syrup
⅓ cup evaporated milk
18 ounces semisweet chocolate chips
¾ cup powdered sugar
⅓ cup crunchy peanut butter
2 teaspoons vanilla
⅓ cup creamy peanut butter

··

In saucepan, combine corn syrup and evaporated milk. Stir until well blended. Cook over medium heat until mixture boils. Remove from heat immediately. Stir in chocolate chips. Cook slowly over low heat, stirring constantly until chips are melted. Remove from heat. Stir in powdered sugar, crunchy peanut butter, and vanilla. Beat until thick and glossy. Spread into 8x8-inch pan lined with foil. Spoon creamy peanut butter onto fudge mixture and swirl to marbleize. Refrigerate overnight.

MARBLED TRUFFLES

¾ cup white chocolate chips
½ cup whipping cream, divided
1 teaspoon vanilla
¾ cup semisweet chocolate chips
1 tablespoon butter
1 teaspoon orange extract
¾ cup powdered sugar

In saucepan over low heat, melt white chocolate
chips, ¼ cup whipping cream, and vanilla, stirring
constantly. Pour into 9x9-inch pan. Refrigerate.
In saucepan, melt semisweet chips, butter, and
remaining whipping cream over low heat, stirring
constantly. Remove from heat. Add extract.
Pour chocolate mixture over refrigerated white
chocolate mixture. Refrigerate until mixture is
thick but soft, about 1 hour. Shape mixture into
1-inch balls. Place powdered sugar in shallow pan.
Roll balls in sugar. Place on waxed paper. Store in
refrigerator.

KEEPING IT SMOOTH

When melting chocolate on the stove or in the microwave, always use dry, room temperature chocolate. Refrigerated chocolate can form condensation as it melts, and even a small drop of water can cause chocolate to seize, or tighten up and form an unworkable mass.

If your chocolate does seize, just add a few drops of vegetable oil. It will help the chocolate to relax and return to a smoother consistency.

Quick Tip

PEPPERMINT PIECES

16 ounces white chocolate chips
4 ounces peppermint candy canes, crushed

....

In small saucepan over low heat, melt white
chocolate chips, stirring until smooth. Add crushed
peppermint. Pour mixture onto waxed paper-lined
baking sheet. Freeze until set. Break into pieces.

Bars & Cookies

My meditation of him shall be sweet:
*I will be glad in the L*ORD.

P*SALM* 104:34 *KJV*

FAVORITE CHOCOLATE CHIP COOKIES

¾ cup shortening
⅔ cup butter (no substitutions)
1 cup sugar
1 cup brown sugar
2 eggs
2 teaspoons vanilla
3 cups flour
1 teaspoon baking soda
1 teaspoon salt
1 (12 ounce) package semisweet chocolate chips

Preheat oven to 375 degrees. Cream shortening, butter, sugars, eggs, and vanilla. Add flour, baking soda, and salt. Mix in chocolate chips. Drop 1-inch spoonfuls on ungreased cookie sheet and bake for approximately 8 minutes or until golden brown.

NO-BAKE COOKIES

2 cups sugar
¼ cup cocoa
¼ cup butter
½ cup milk
½ cup peanut butter
1 teaspoon vanilla
2½ cups oats
½ cup flaked coconut

....

In large saucepan, boil sugar, cocoa, butter, and milk for 1 minute. Remove from heat and stir in peanut butter, vanilla, oats, and coconut. Drop spoonfuls onto waxed paper to harden. Let cool.

SEVEN-LAYER BARS

½ cup butter or margarine
1 cup graham cracker crumbs
1 cup semisweet chocolate chips
1 cup butterscotch chips
1 cup chopped walnuts
1 cup shredded coconut
1 (14 ounce) can sweetened condensed milk

Preheat oven to 350 degrees. In 9x13-inch baking dish, cut butter and melt in oven. Remove dish before butter turns brown. Sprinkle graham cracker crumbs on top. Pat down. Scatter chips, nuts, and coconut in layers on top. Drizzle with condensed milk. Bake for 30 minutes or until light brown.

CHOCOLATE MACAROONS

1 (18.25 ounce) package chocolate cake mix
⅓ cup butter, softened
2 eggs, divided
1 (14 ounce) can sweetened condensed milk
1 teaspoon vanilla extract
1 (12 ounce) package semisweet chocolate chips
1⅓ cups flaked, sweetened coconut, divided
½ cup walnuts, chopped

Preheat oven to 350 degrees. In a large bowl, combine cake mix, butter, and 1 egg until mixture is crumbly. Press firmly into a greased 9x13-inch baking pan. In a medium bowl, combine condensed milk, 1 egg, and vanilla extract; stir in the chocolate chips, 1 cup coconut, and walnuts. Spread over mixture in baking pan. Top with remaining coconut. Bake for 30 to 40 minutes or until golden brown. Cool completely in pan before cutting into bars.

PEANUT BUTTER CHOCOLATE KISSES

1 cup butter, softened
1 cup peanut butter
1 cup sugar
1 cup brown sugar
2 eggs
2 teaspoons vanilla
3½ cups flour
2 teaspoons baking soda
1 teaspoon salt
Additional sugar
1 (16 ounce) package chocolate candy kisses,
   unwrapped

....

Combine butter, peanut butter, and sugars; blend until creamy. Add eggs and vanilla; blend. Mix flour, baking soda, and salt. Add to creamed mixture; mix well. Shape dough into balls and roll in additional sugar. Bake at 350 degrees for 7 minutes. Let cookies set on trays for 2 to 3 minutes after removing from oven. Then press unwrapped kiss in center of each cookie and move to cooling rack.

MERINGUE KISSES

2 egg whites
$\frac{1}{8}$ teaspoon salt
$\frac{2}{3}$ cup powdered sugar
$\frac{2}{3}$ cup semisweet chocolate chips
$\frac{1}{3}$ cup chopped pecans

In a mixing bowl, beat egg whites until foamy. Add salt, then gradually add sugar, one tablespoon at a time, beating until very stiff peaks form. Fold in chocolate chips and pecans. Drop by teaspoonfuls onto lightly greased cookie sheets. Put in a preheated 350-degree oven and turn off heat. Leave overnight. These are best served fresh the next day.

CHOCOLATE CHIP BLOND BROWNIES

BARS & COOKIES

2 cups brown sugar
²/₃ cup butter, melted
2 eggs
2 teaspoons vanilla
1 to 2 cups flour
1 teaspoon baking powder
¼ teaspoon baking soda
¼ teaspoon salt
½ cup nuts, chopped
Semisweet chocolate chips

Add brown sugar to melted butter; cool. Add eggs and vanilla to mixture and blend well. In separate bowl, sift flour, baking powder, baking soda, and salt. Add gradually to sugar mixture. Stir in chopped nuts if desired. Pour mixture into greased 8x12-inch baking pan. Sprinkle chocolate chips on top. Bake at 350 degrees for 20 to 25 minutes. (Do not overcook.) Cut into squares.

STORING CHOCOLATE

Make sure the chocolate you buy isn't stored in or around very aromatic foods like garlic, tea, coffee, or detergents. These strong scents can affect the flavor of exposed chocolate.

CHOCOLATE OATMEAL SANDWICH COOKIES

2½ cups plus 2 tablespoons butter, softened
1 cup sugar
1½ cups brown sugar
2 eggs
4 teaspoons vanilla, divided
2½ cups flour
½ cup cocoa
2 teaspoons baking soda
1 teaspoon salt
6 cups quick oats
1 (12 ounce) package semisweet chocolate chips
1 (14 ounce) can sweetened condensed milk

••

Preheat oven to 375 degrees. Beat 2½ cups butter and sugars until fluffy. Beat in eggs and 3 teaspoons vanilla. Combine flour, cocoa, baking soda, and salt. Add to creamed mixture. Stir in oats. Drop by tablespoons onto ungreased cookie sheets. Bake for 10 minutes. Cool. In saucepan, combine chips, condensed milk, 2 tablespoons butter, and 1 teaspoon vanilla. Over medium heat, cook and stir until chips are melted. Immediately spread filling between cooled cookies.

CHOCOLATE SYRUP BROWNIES

½ cup butter or margarine, softened
1 cup sugar
4 eggs
1 (16 ounce) bottle chocolate-flavored syrup
1¼ cups flour
1 cup walnuts, chopped

Quick frosting:
⅔ cup sugar
3 tablespoons milk
3 tablespoons butter
½ cup semisweet chocolate chips

Cream butter and sugar; beat in eggs. Blend in syrup and flour; stir in nuts. Pour into greased 9x13-inch baking pan. Bake at 350 degrees for 30 to 35 minutes. Cool slightly before frosting. Quick frosting: Mix sugar, milk, and butter; bring to a boil and boil for 30 seconds. Remove from heat; stir in chocolate chips until melted. Frosting will be thin. Spread over brownies and cut into bars.

TRIPLE CHIP WONDER COOKIES

1 box white cake mix
1 stick butter or margarine, melted
2 eggs
½ cup white chocolate chips
½ cup butterscotch chips
½ cup semisweet chocolate chips

Mix cake mix with melted butter and eggs. Stir in chips. Drop spoonfuls onto ungreased cookie sheet. Bake for 6 to 7 minutes at 350 degrees. Do not overbake; cookies will set up as they cool.

CHOCOLATE CRINKLES

1 box chocolate cake mix
1 large egg
¼ cup oil
¼ cup water
1 cup semisweet chocolate chips
2 cups powdered sugar

Preheat oven to 350 degrees. Combine cake mix, egg, oil, and water. Beat until well blended. Stir in chocolate chips. Shape into balls and roll in powdered sugar. Place about 1 inch apart on greased cookie sheet. Bake for 12 to 15 minutes. Sprinkle with additional powdered sugar.

CARAMEL CHOCOLATE PECAN BARS

¾ cup butter
¾ cup sugar
1 cup flour
1 cup quick oats
½ teaspoon baking soda
¼ teaspoon salt

1 (14 ounce) package caramels
⅓ cup evaporated milk
½ cup chopped pecans
1 cup semisweet chocolate chips

Preheat oven to 350 degrees. Beat butter and sugar until fluffy. Combine flour, oats, baking soda, and salt and add to butter mixture until crumbly. Do not overmix. Reserve 1 cup crust mixture and press remainder in ungreased 9x13-inch pan. Bake for 10 minutes. Cool in pan for 10 minutes. In saucepan, cook caramels and evaporated milk over low heat until caramels melt and mixture is smooth. Spread over baked cookie crust. Sprinkle with pecans then with reserved crumbs and chocolate chips. Bake for 15 to 20 minutes or until top crumbs are golden. Cool in pan on wire rack. Cut into bars. Makes 32.

CHOCOLATE ALMOND TEA CAKES

¾ cup margarine or butter, softened
⅓ cup powdered sugar
1 cup flour
½ cup instant cocoa mix
½ cup toasted almonds, diced
Additional powdered sugar

Combine margarine and ⅓ cup powdered sugar. Stir in flour, cocoa mix, and almonds. (Refrigerate until firm if dough is too soft to shape.) Heat oven to 325 degrees. Shape dough into 1-inch balls and place on ungreased cookie sheets. Bake for about 20 minutes or until set. Dip tops into powdered sugar while still warm. Let cool and dip again.

WHITE CHOCOLATE MACADAMIA NUT COOKIES

2 cups flour
1 teaspoon baking soda
1 teaspoon cream of tartar
½ teaspoon salt
1 stick salted butter, softened
½ cup shortening
½ cup sugar
½ cup brown sugar
1 egg
1 teaspoon vanilla
6 ounces white chocolate chips
½ cup coarsely chopped macadamia nuts, toasted
Additional sugar

....

Combine flour, baking soda, cream of tartar, and salt. Cream butter, shortening, sugars, egg, and vanilla. Gradually add flour mixture. Stir in white chocolate chips and nuts. Refrigerate for 1 hour. Preheat oven to 400 degrees. Shape dough into 1-inch balls and roll in sugar. Place on ungreased cookie sheet; flatten slightly. Bake for 8 to 10 minutes. Remove from cookie sheet immediately. Makes about 5 dozen cookies.

CHOCOLATE AND PEANUT BUTTER BARS

2 cups flour
¾ cup cocoa
1 teaspoon baking soda
1¼ cups butter, softened
2 cups sugar
2 eggs
2 teaspoons vanilla
½ cup semisweet chocolate chips
1 cup peanut butter chips

....

Preheat oven to 350 degrees. Grease jelly roll pan. In small bowl, stir together flour, cocoa, and baking soda. In large bowl, beat butter and sugar until fluffy. Add eggs and vanilla; beat well. Gradually add flour mixture, beating well. Stir in chocolate and peanut butter chips. Spread batter into prepared pan. Bake for 20 minutes or until set in middle. Do not overbake. Cool completely in pan; cut into bars.

SELECTING THE BEST CHOCOLATE

The qualities to look for in good chocolate are a glossy, unblemished surface and a clean snap when broken. Try to avoid chocolate that has a dusty white film on it (called "bloom") as this indicates the chocolate has been improperly stored or has melted and rehardened. Poor quality chocolate will crumble when broken.

Quick
Tip

BANANA CHOCOLATE CHIP COOKIES

²/₃ cup shortening
1 cup sugar
2 eggs
1 teaspoon vanilla
2¼ cups flour
2 teaspoons baking powder
¼ teaspoon baking soda
½ teaspoon salt
3 small ripe bananas, mashed
1 (12 ounce) package milk chocolate chips

. . . .

Preheat oven to 400 degrees. Blend shortening
and sugar. Add eggs one at a time, beating
after each addition. Add vanilla. Combine dry
ingredients and add to creamed mixture. Add
mashed bananas and mix well. Stir in chocolate
chips. Drop by teaspoonful onto ungreased cookie
sheet. Bake for 12 to 15 minutes. Makes 6 dozen.

CHOCOLATE CINNAMON BARS

2 cups flour
1 teaspoon baking powder
1 ½ cups sugar, divided
1 tablespoon and 1 teaspoon cinnamon, divided
½ cup butter, softened
½ cup shortening
1 egg, beaten
1 egg, separated
1 cup semisweet chocolate chips
½ cup pecans, chopped

Preheat oven to 350 degrees. Lightly grease a 10x15-inch jelly roll pan; set aside. In a large bowl, combine flour, baking powder, 1 cup sugar, and 1 tablespoon cinnamon. Add butter, shortening, beaten egg, and egg yolk; mix well. Press into prepared pan. Beat egg white slightly; brush over mixture in pan. In a small bowl combine ½ cup sugar, 1 teaspoon cinnamon, chocolate chips, and pecans. Sprinkle mixture over top. Bake for 25 minutes. Allow to cool completely before cutting into bars.

ALMOND ROCA BARS

1 cup butter
1/2 cup sugar
1/2 cup brown sugar
1 egg, beaten
1 teaspoon vanilla
1/2 teaspoon almond extract
2 cups minus 2 tablespoons flour
1 (12 ounce) bag semisweet chocolate chips
1 small package slivered or roasted almonds

Preheat oven to 350 degrees. Cream butter and sugars. Add remaining ingredients except chocolate chips and almonds. Mix thoroughly and spread on large cookie sheet. Bake 10 to 12 minutes. Melt chocolate chips in microwave for 30 seconds. Stir. Repeat until creamy. Spread over warm cookie and sprinkle slivered almonds on top. Cut into bars when cool.

CHOCOLATE LACE COOKIES

⅔ cup butter, melted
2 cups quick oats
1 cup sugar
⅔ cup flour
¼ cup light corn syrup
¼ cup milk
1 teaspoon vanilla
¼ teaspoon salt
2 cups milk chocolate chips

Preheat oven to 375 degrees. Combine butter, oats, sugar, flour, corn syrup, milk, vanilla, and salt; mix well. Drop by teaspoons onto foil-lined cookie sheets. Flatten each cookie until thin with rubber spatula. Bake for 5 to 7 minutes. Let cool. Peel foil away from cookies and let cool. Melt chocolate chips in microwave for 30 seconds. Stir. Repeat until smooth. Spread chocolate on flat side of half the cookies. Top with remaining cookies.

CHOCOLATE CHEESECAKE COOKIE BARS

2 tubes refrigerated chocolate chip cookie dough
1 (12 ounce) package milk chocolate chips
2 (8 ounce) packages cream cheese
2 eggs
1 teaspoon vanilla

....

Preheat oven to 350 degrees. Grease 9x13-inch pan. Press 1 tube of cookie dough evenly into pan, forming crust. Melt chocolate chips in microwave for 30 seconds. Stir. Repeat until creamy. Blend cream cheese, eggs, and vanilla until smooth. Fold in melted chocolate. Layer over dough in pan. Cut second tube of cookie dough in $1/4$-inch slices. Place on top of chocolate cream cheese mixture. Cover completely to form top crust. Bake for 30 minutes. Chill and refrigerate or freeze before serving.

KEY LIME WHITE CHOCOLATE CHIP COOKIES

½ cup butter, softened
1 cup sugar
1 egg
1 egg yolk
1½ cups flour
1 teaspoon baking powder
½ teaspoon salt
¼ cup lime juice
1½ teaspoons lime zest
¾ cup white chocolate chips

Preheat oven to 350 degrees. In a large bowl, cream together butter, sugar, egg, and egg yolk. Blend in the flour, baking powder, salt, lime juice, and lime zest. Fold in chocolate chips. Roll dough into walnut-sized balls. Place on ungreased baking sheets and bake for 8 to 10 minutes.

CHOCOLATE CHIP PUMPKIN COOKIES

1 teaspoon baking soda
1 teaspoon milk
1 cup pumpkin
¾ cup sugar
½ cup vegetable oil
1 egg
2 cups flour
2 teaspoons baking powder
1 teaspoon cinnamon
½ teaspoon salt
1 cup semisweet chocolate chips
1 teaspoon vanilla

. . . .

Preheat oven to 375 degrees. Dissolve baking soda in milk and set aside. Combine pumpkin, sugar, oil, and egg; stir. Add flour, baking powder, cinnamon, salt, and baking soda mixture. Mix well. Stir in chocolate chips and vanilla. Spoon onto cookie sheet. Bake for 10 to 12 minutes. Be careful not to overbake. Cookies will be soft and moist.

DOUBLE CHOCOLATE MUD BARS

½ cup butter, softened
1 cup sugar
2 large eggs, separated
1½ cups flour
1 teaspoon baking powder
½ teaspoon salt
1 cup walnuts, chopped
½ cup semisweet chocolate chips
1 cup miniature marshmallows
1 cup candy-coated chocolate pieces (optional)
1 cup brown sugar

....

Beat together butter and sugar. Beat egg yolks one at a time. In separate bowl, mix together flour, baking powder, and salt. Fold flour mixture into butter mixture. Press into greased 9x13-inch baking pan. Sprinkle with nuts, chocolate chips, marshmallows, and, if desired, candy-coated chocolate pieces. Beat egg whites at high speed until stiff peaks form. Fold in brown sugar. Spread over mixture in pan. Bake at 350 degrees for 35 minutes. Cool completely; cut into squares.

KNOW YOUR CHOCOLATE

*Unsweetened Chocolate is pure, unadulterated cocoa, also known as bitter or baking chocolate.

*Semisweet and Dark Chocolate is pure cocoa to which sugar and other ingredients have been added. The bitterness of a particular variety depends on the percentage of pure chocolate it contains. The more pure chocolate, the more bitter it will be.

*Milk Chocolate is pure cocoa mixed with sugar and condensed milk to give it its signature rich sweetness. It's used to make most candy bars.

*White Chocolate isn't a true chocolate because it isn't made from cocoa beans. But it does contain cocoa butter, which gives it its smooth, creamy texture.

BARS & COOKIES

BONBON KISSES

1 (12 ounce) package semisweet chocolate chips
1/4 cup butter
1 (14 ounce) can sweetened condensed milk
2 cups flour
1 teaspoon vanilla
30 milk chocolate candy kisses, unwrapped
30 chocolate-striped candy kisses, unwrapped
2 ounces white chocolate chips

Preheat oven to 350 degrees. In medium saucepan, combine semisweet chocolate chips and butter; cook and stir over very low heat until smooth. Add condensed milk; mix well. Combine flour, chocolate mixture, and vanilla; mix well. Shape 1 tablespoon dough around each candy kiss, covering completely. Place on ungreased cookie sheets. Bake at 350 degrees for 6 to 8 minutes. Do not overbake. Remove from cookie sheets and let cool. Melt white chocolate chips in microwave for 30 seconds. Stir. Repeat until smooth and creamy. Drizzle over cookies with fork. Store in covered container. Makes 5 dozen.

Pies & Cakes

For thou shalt eat the labour of thine hands: happy shalt thou be, and it shall be well with thee.
PSALM 128:2

CHOCOLATE CHEESECAKE

½ cup butter or margarine, melted
1½ cups graham cracker crumbs
½ cup sugar
⅔ cup water
1 envelope gelatin, unflavored
2 (8 ounce) packages cream cheese, softened
4 (1 ounce) squares semisweet chocolate, melted
1 (14 ounce) can sweetened condensed milk
1 teaspoon vanilla
1 cup frozen whipped topping, thawed

. . . .

In 9-inch springform pan, mix together butter, graham cracker crumbs, and sugar. Press firmly on bottom of pan (do not line sides). Pour water into small saucepan. Sprinkle gelatin over water and let stand for 1 minute. Over low heat, stir until gelatin dissolves; set aside. In large bowl, beat cream cheese and chocolate until fluffy. Gradually beat in sweetened condensed milk. Add vanilla and beat until smooth. Stir gelatin mixture into cream cheese mixture. Fold in whipped topping. Pour mixture into prepared pan. Chill in refrigerator for 3 hours or until set. Garnish with whipped topping. Keep refrigerated.

ÉCLAIR CAKE

1 box graham crackers
4 cups milk
2 small boxes instant vanilla pudding mix
1 (16 ounce) container frozen whipped topping,
      thawed
1 (16 ounce) tub prepared chocolate frosting

Line bottom of 9x13-inch baking pan with graham crackers. In large bowl, combine milk and pudding mix according to directions on box. Fold in whipped topping. Spread layer of pudding mixture over graham crackers. Alternate graham cracker and pudding layers to top of pan. In microwave, heat tub of prepared frosting, uncovered, for 1 minute on 50% power. Pour over cake. Refrigerate for at least 12 hours before serving.

CHOCOLATE TRUFFLE CAKE

1 (12 ounce) package semisweet chocolate chips, divided
½ cup whipping cream
4 eggs
½ cup sugar
¼ cup flour
1 cup frozen whipped topping, thawed

....

Preheat oven to 325 degrees. Reserve ⅛ cup chocolate chips and place remaining chips in large microwavable bowl. Add cream. Microwave on high for 2 minutes or until chocolate is almost melted. Stir until chocolate is completely melted; cool slightly. Add eggs, sugar, and flour; beat with whisk until well blended. Pour into lightly greased 9-inch pie pan. Bake for 35 minutes or until outer half of pie is puffed and center is slightly soft; cool. Top with whipped topping just before serving.

PIES & CAKES

CHOCOLATE BROWNIE CAKE

1 (18.25 ounce) package devil's food cake mix
1 (3.9 ounce) package instant chocolate
  pudding mix
4 eggs
1 cup sour cream
½ cup vegetable oil
½ cup water
2 cups semisweet chocolate chips
1 (16 ounce) can chocolate frosting

. . . .

Preheat oven to 350 degrees. Grease and flour a
10-inch Bundt pan. In a large bowl, stir together
cake mix and pudding mix. Make a well in the
center and pour in eggs, sour cream, oil, and water.
Beat with an electric mixer on low speed until
well blended. Scrape bowl, and beat 4 minutes on
medium speed. Stir in chocolate chips. Pour batter
into prepared pan. Bake for 50 to 60 minutes
or until a toothpick inserted into the center
comes out clean. Allow to cool completely before
frosting.

3-LAYER CHOCOLATE CAKE

3 sticks butter
2½ cups sugar
6 eggs
3 cups flour, sifted and divided
1½ teaspoons baking powder, divided
1 teaspoon salt, divided
2 cups whole milk, divided
1 tablespoon lemon juice
2 tablespoons vanilla
1 large tub chocolate frosting

Preheat oven to 350 degrees. Grease three 9-inch cake pans and dust with flour. Set aside. In large mixing bowl, cream butter. Add sugar, mix well. Add eggs one at a time, mix well. Add 1½ cups flour with half of baking powder and half of salt with 1 cup of milk; mix well. Add remaining flour, salt, and baking powder with remainder of milk; mix well. Add lemon juice and vanilla and blend 3 minutes. Pour batter into cake pans and cook 30 to 40 minutes, until cake tests done. Let stand on counter for 5 minutes. Remove from pans and cool on wire rack. To assemble cake, put 1 layer on cake plate and frost. Repeat.

CHOCOLATE TURTLE CHEESECAKE

1 (7 ounce) package caramels
¼ cup evaporated milk
½ cup pecans, chopped
1 (9-inch) prepared chocolate crumb piecrust
2 (3 ounce) packages cream cheese, softened
½ cup sour cream
1¼ cups milk
1 (3.9 ounce) package chocolate instant pudding
½ cup fudge topping
¼ cup pecans, chopped

Place caramels and evaporated milk in large saucepan. Heat over medium heat, stirring constantly until smooth. Stir in ½ cup pecans. Pour into piecrust. Combine cream cheese, sour cream, milk, and pudding mix in blender. Process until smooth. Pour pudding mixture over caramel layer, covering evenly. Loosely cover pie and chill until set. Drizzle fudge topping over pudding layer in decorative pattern. Sprinkle with ¼ cup pecans. Cover loosely and chill in refrigerator.

CHOCOLATE CHIP CHEESECAKE

1 ½ cups chocolate sandwich cookie crumbs
3 tablespoons butter, melted
3 (3 ounce) packages cream cheese, softened
1 (14 ounce) can sweetened condensed milk
2 teaspoons vanilla
3 eggs
1 cup semisweet chocolate chips, divided
1 teaspoon flour

Combine cookie crumbs and butter; press into 9-inch springform pan. Beat cream cheese until fluffy, then beat in milk, vanilla, and eggs. Toss ½ cup chocolate chips with flour to coat; stir into cream cheese mixture. Pour into prepared pan and sprinkle with remaining chips. Bake at 300 degrees for 1 hour or until cake springs back when lightly touched. Cool. Chill. Serve.

Experiment with various cheese grater surfaces and vegetable peelers to create different kinds of chocolate flakes and curls to garnish your chocolaty treats.

Quick Tip

WHITE CHOCOLATE CHEESECAKE

3 (8 ounce) packages cream cheese, softened
¾ cup sugar
¼ cup flour
3 eggs
4 ounces white chocolate
½ teaspoon vanilla
1½ cups heavy whipping cream

....

Preheat oven to 300 degrees. Wrap outside of
10-inch springform pan with foil. Grease inside
of pan. In mixing bowl, beat cream cheese, sugar,
and flour until light and fluffy. Beat in eggs one at a
time, mixing well after each addition. Scrape bowl.
Melt white chocolate. With electric mixer on low
speed, mix melted white chocolate into cream
cheese mixture. Slowly beat in vanilla and cream.
Blend well. Pour mixture into prepared springform
pan. Place pan in water bath filled with warm
water. Bake for 50 to 60 minutes or until center of
cheesecake is just firm. Cool at room temperature
for 1 hour. Refrigerate until set before removing
from pan.

CHOCOLATE PIE

3 (1 ounce) squares semisweet chocolate
1 (14 ounce) can sweetened condensed milk
¼ teaspoon salt
¼ cup hot water
2 egg yolks
1 teaspoon vanilla
1 cup frozen whipped topping, thawed
1 (9-inch) prepared pie crust
Additional whipped topping
Chocolate shavings

....

In large saucepan, combine chocolate, sweetened condensed milk, and salt. Cook over medium heat until thick and bubbly, stirring constantly. Add water and egg yolks, stirring quickly until mixture is thick and bubbly again. Remove from heat and stir in vanilla. Allow to cool for 15 minutes. Chill in refrigerator for an additional 20 to 30 minutes; stir. Fold whipped topping into cooled chocolate mixture; stir. Pour chocolate mixture into prepared piecrust. Cool for 2½ to 3 hours or until chocolate is set. Cover with additional whipped topping. Garnish with chocolate shavings. Keep refrigerated.

EARTHQUAKE CAKE

1 cup nuts, chopped
1 cup flaked coconut, finely chopped
1 German chocolate cake mix
1 (8 ounce) package cream cheese, softened
1 cup shortening
1 pound powdered sugar

Grease 9x13-inch baking pan; put nuts and coconut in pan. Prepare cake mix according to package directions and spread on top of nuts and coconut. Then beat together cream cheese, shortening, and powdered sugar until fluffy. Drop by spoonfuls on top of cake batter in pan. Bake at 350 degrees for 40 minutes or until done when tested.

FILLED CHOCOLATE CUPCAKES

1 (18.5 ounce) package chocolate cake mix,
   prepared according to directions
1 (8 ounce) package cream cheese, softened
½ cup sugar
1 egg
1 cup semisweet chocolate chips
1 (16 ounce) can cream cheese frosting

Preheat oven to 350 degrees. Line muffin pans
with paper liners; set aside. Prepare chocolate
cake mix according to directions, set aside. In
a separate bowl, cream together cream cheese
and sugar until smooth. Beat in egg; stir until well
blended. Stir in chocolate chips. Fill muffin cups
⅓ full with chocolate cake batter. Add 1 teaspoon
cream cheese mixture to center; top with more
cake batter until ⅔ full. Repeat until batter is
finished. Bake cupcakes according to package
directions. Allow to cool completely before
frosting.

CHOCOLATE POUND CAKE

1 box chocolate cake mix
1 small box instant chocolate pudding
1¾ cups milk
2 eggs
1 bag mini chocolate chips
Powdered sugar

Preheat oven to 350 degrees. In large bowl, combine all ingredients except powdered sugar and beat by hand. Bake for 1 hour. Dust with powdered sugar.

OATMEAL CHOCOLATE CHIP CAKE

1¾ cups boiling water
1 cup oats
1 cup brown sugar
1 cup sugar
½ cup margarine
2 eggs
1¾ cups flour
1 teaspoon baking soda
½ teaspoon salt
1 tablespoon cocoa
1 cup semisweet chocolate chips, divided
¾ cup walnuts, chopped

....

Preheat oven to 350 degrees. Pour boiling water over oats; let stand at room temperature for 10 minutes. Add sugars and margarine to oatmeal. Stir until margarine melts. Add eggs and mix well. Then add flour, baking soda, salt, and cocoa, stirring until well blended. Add half of chocolate chips. Pour batter into greased 9x13-inch baking pan. Sprinkle nuts and remaining chocolate chips on top. Bake 40 minutes.

POPCORN CAKE

4 quarts popped popcorn
½ cup candy-coated chocolate pieces
1 cup chopped nuts
1½ pounds mini marshmallows
¼ cup vegetable oil
½ cup butter

Combine popcorn, candy-coated chocolate pieces, and nuts in large bowl; mix well. In saucepan, combine marshmallows, oil, and butter. Cook until marshmallows and butter are melted, stirring constantly. Pour over popcorn mixture. Pat into greased Bundt pan. Turn upside down onto plate until cake releases.

SOUR CREAM CHOCOLATE CHIP CAKE

6 tablespoons butter, softened
1 cup sugar
2 eggs
1 1/3 cups flour
1 1/2 teaspoons baking powder
1 teaspoon baking soda
1 teaspoon ground cinnamon
1 cup sour cream
1 cup mini semisweet chocolate chips
1 tablespoon sugar

Mix butter and sugar until blended. Beat in eggs one at a time. In separate bowl, stir baking powder, baking soda, and cinnamon into flour, then blend with creamed mixture. Mix in sour cream. Pour batter into greased and floured 8x10-inch baking pan. Scatter chocolate chips evenly over batter. Then sprinkle 1 tablespoon sugar over top. Bake at 350 degrees for 35 minutes or until cake just begins to pull away from sides of pan.

WHAT'S THE DIFFERENCE?

When it comes to cocoa powder, you have two options: natural and Dutch–processed. Natural cocoa is red-brown in color and usually labeled unsweetened cocoa powder. Dutch-processed, on the other hand, is much darker and less acidic.

Quick Tip

You can typically use whatever kind of cocoa you'd like interchangeably, but using very dark Dutch–processed cocoa in recipes that include baking soda may result in a "soapy" flavor as a result of the Dutch–processed cocoa's high alkalinity.

FUDGY PECAN PIE

2 squares semisweet chocolate
¼ cup butter
1 (14 ounce) can sweetened condensed milk
½ cup hot water
2 eggs, well beaten
1¼ cups pecan pieces
1 teaspoon vanilla
¼ teaspoon salt
1 unbaked piecrust

Preheat oven to 350 degrees. In saucepan over low heat, melt chocolate and butter. Stir in milk, hot water, and eggs; mix well. Remove from heat; stir in pecans, vanilla, and salt. Pour into piecrust. Bake for 40 minutes or until center is set. Cool on wire rack. Serve pie warm or chilled. Store covered in refrigerator.

WHITE CHOCOLATE PIE

1 (12 ounce) package white chocolate chips
1/2 cup whipping cream
1/4 cup butter
2 teaspoons light corn syrup
1 (10 ounce) bag frozen raspberries, thawed
1 (10-inch) baked pie shell

Microwave chips until melted. In saucepan, combine whipping cream, butter, and corn syrup. Bring to a boil, stirring constantly. Pour over chocolate; stir until blended and smooth. Stir in raspberries. Spoon into pie shell. Chill until firm.

CHOCOLATE RASPBERRY CHEESE PIE

2 (3 ounce) packages cream cheese, softened
1 (14 ounce) can sweetened condensed milk
1 egg
3 tablespoons lemon juice
1 teaspoon vanilla extract
1 cup fresh or frozen raspberries
1 (9-inch) chocolate piecrust
2 (1 ounce) squares semisweet baking chocolate
¼ cup whipping cream

Preheat oven to 350 degrees. In a large bowl, beat cream cheese until fluffy. Gradually beat in condensed milk until smooth. Add egg, lemon juice, and vanilla; mix well. Arrange raspberries on bottom of crust. Slowly pour cheese mixture over fruit. Bake for 30 to 35 minutes or until center is almost set. Cool. In a small saucepan over low heat, melt chocolate with whipping cream. Cook and stir until thickened and smooth. Remove from heat. Top cheesecake with chocolate glaze. Allow to chill before serving.

FRENCH SILK CHOCOLATE PIE

1 cup butter
1½ cups sugar
4 tablespoons unsweetened cocoa powder
2 teaspoons vanilla extract
4 eggs
1 (9-inch) baked piecrust

In a large bowl, cream together the butter and sugar. Blend in the cocoa and vanilla. With an electric mixer on high speed, beat in one egg until thoroughly blended. Repeat with each remaining egg. Keep whipping until fluffy. Spread mixture into the prepared pie shell. Refrigerate until chilled. Top with whipped topping if desired.

CHOCOLATE ALMOND PIE

½ cup milk
16 large marshmallows
6 chocolate-almond candy bars
1 cup whipping cream, whipped
1 (9-inch) piecrust, baked and cooled
Whipped topping
Chocolate curls

Heat milk in saucepan until hot; dissolve marshmallows in hot milk. Break and add candy bars. Stir until melted. Remove from heat and cool. Fold in 1 cup whipped cream. Pour into baked 9-inch piecrust. Refrigerate until set. Serve with sweetened whipped cream and chocolate curls.

CHOCOLATE PEANUT BUTTER PIE

2 cups extra crunchy peanut butter
1 (8 ounce) package cream cheese, softened
2 cups powdered sugar
1 cup milk
3 (8 ounce) containers frozen whipped topping,
   thawed and divided
3 (9 inch) prepared chocolate crumb piecrusts

Mix peanut butter and cream cheese until
smooth. Add powdered sugar, milk, and 12
ounces (1½ containers) whipped topping. Blend
thoroughly and pour into piecrusts, spreading
evenly. Top each pie with 4 ounces whipped
topping. (These pies freeze and keep well.)

CHOCOLATE BAR PIE

4 ounces cream cheese, softened

1 tablespoon and 1¾ cups milk, divided

2 (12 ounce) containers frozen whipped topping, thawed and divided

2 (2.7 ounce) chocolate-covered caramel peanut nougat candy bars, chopped

1 (3.9 ounce) package instant chocolate pudding mix

1 (9-inch) chocolate piecrust

In a large bowl, mix cream cheese and 1 tablespoon milk with wire whisk until smooth. Gently stir in 2 cups whipped topping and chopped candy bars; set aside. In a medium bowl, add 1¾ cups milk and pudding mix. Beat with wire whisk for 1 minute. Gently stir in ½ cup whipped topping. Spread half of the pudding mixture on bottom of crust. Spread cream cheese mixture over pudding mixture. Top with remaining pudding mixture. Refrigerate for 4 hours or until pie is set. Garnish with remaining whipped topping.

COOKIES AND CREAM PIE

1 (3.9 ounce) package chocolate instant pudding, prepared
1 (8 ounce) container frozen whipped topping, thawed
1½ cups chocolate sandwich cookie crumbs
1 (9-inch) prepared chocolate crumb piecrust

Prepare pudding according to pie filling directions on package; allow to set. When pudding is ready, fold in whipped topping. Add cookie crumbs; stir. Pour mixture into prepared piecrust. Freeze pie until firm. Thaw in refrigerator before serving.

THE PERFECT MELTING POINT

When melting chocolate on a stovetop, use a confectionary thermometer. Chocolate is very sensitive to high temperatures. Dark chocolate should never be heated above 120 degrees, while milk and white chocolates should never be heated above 110 degrees. Overheated chocolate can become thick and difficult to work with.

Quick Tip

If your chocolate does overheat, cool it quickly by removing it from the heat source and stirring in a handful of unmelted chocolate chunks. If it's still too thick, try adding a teaspoon of vegetable oil to achieve a smoother consistency.

CHOCOLATE CHIP ROCKY ROAD PIE

½ cup butter
1 cup brown sugar, packed
1 egg, slightly beaten
2 tablespoons hot water
1 teaspoon vanilla
1 cup flour, sifted
½ teaspoon baking powder
¼ teaspoon salt
⅛ teaspoon baking soda
½ cup nuts, chopped
1 cup mini semisweet chocolate chips, divided
1 cup miniature marshmallows, divided

Melt butter over low heat; mix in brown sugar until well blended. Add egg, hot water, and vanilla. In separate bowl, stir together flour, baking powder, salt, and baking soda. Add to sugar mixture; mix well. Mix in nuts, half of chocolate chips, and half of marshmallows. Spread mixture into two 9-inch pie plates. Sprinkle with remaining chips and marshmallows. Bake at 350 degrees for 20 minutes. Cool.

Breads & Breakfast Treats

Weeping may endure for a night, but joy cometh in the morning.
PSALM 30:5

CHOCOLATE BREAD

2½ cups flour
1½ teaspoons baking soda
½ cup cocoa
1 cup sugar
1 egg, beaten
⅓ cup butter, melted
1¼ cups milk
¾ cup chopped walnuts

Preheat oven to 350 degrees. In large mixing bowl, sift together flour, baking soda, cocoa, and sugar. In smaller bowl, mix together egg, butter, and milk. Pour wet ingredients into dry ingredients; mix well. Fold in walnuts. Pour into greased 5x9-inch loaf pan. Bake for 1 hour.

WHITE CHOCOLATE BREAD

4⅓ cups flour
1 teaspoon yeast
1 teaspoon sugar
2½ cups water
2⅓ cups white chocolate chips

In small bowl, mix flour, yeast, and sugar. Add water and mix 12 minutes on medium speed. Add chips and mix for 2 to 3 minutes more or until chips are well distributed throughout the dough. Lightly knead dough into ball. Let rest for 15 to 20 minutes. Preheat oven to 450 degrees. Cut dough into 4 portions and knead into desired shape. Place in baking pan lined with parchment paper and bake for approximately 20 minutes or until nicely browned.

BANANA BREAD

1 cup sugar
½ cup butter, softened
2 eggs, beaten
3 ripe bananas, mashed
2 cups flour, sifted
1 teaspoon baking soda
1 cup semisweet chocolate chips
½ cup chopped nuts

Preheat oven to 350 degrees. Combine all
ingredients in order listed. Bake in greased 5x9-
inch loaf pan for 1 hour.

CEREAL BREAD

1 cup frosted corn flakes
2 cups milk
2 cups sugar
2 eggs
1 teaspoon vanilla
3½ cups flour
1 teaspoon baking soda
2 teaspoons baking powder
½ cup semisweet chocolate chips

Preheat oven to 350 degrees. Soak cereal in milk for 10 minutes. In large bowl, beat sugar and eggs. Add cereal mixture and vanilla. Sift flour with baking soda and baking powder and stir thoroughly into cereal mixture. Add chocolate chips and mix well. Pour into 2 greased 5x9-inch loaf pans and bake for about 45 minutes or until toothpick inserted in center comes out clean.

PUMPKIN BREAD

½ cup butter
1 cup sugar
2 eggs
1¼ cups canned pumpkin
2 cups flour
1 teaspoon baking soda
1 teaspoon cinnamon
½ teaspoon nutmeg
½ teaspoon pumpkin pie spice
¼ teaspoon cloves
¼ teaspoon ginger
¼ cup semisweet chocolate chips
¼ cup chopped walnuts

Preheat oven to 350 degrees. Grease and flour 5x9-inch loaf pan. In large bowl, cream butter and gradually add sugar, eggs, and pumpkin. Mix well. Combine dry ingredients and stir into creamed mixture, blending well. Stir in chocolate chips and nuts. Bake for 45 to 50 minutes or until toothpick inserted in center comes out clean. Cool on wire rack.

CHOCOLATE ZUCCHINI BREAD

2 cups shredded zucchini
3 eggs
½ cup applesauce
2 cups sugar
½ cup vegetable oil
3¼ cups flour, sifted
½ cup cocoa
3 teaspoons cinnamon
1 teaspoon baking soda
¼ teaspoon baking powder
1 cup semisweet chocolate chips

Preheat oven to 350 degrees. Grease and flour 2 loaf pans. In mixing bowl, mix together zucchini, eggs, applesauce, sugar, and oil. Add remaining ingredients. Divide batter between prepared pans. Bake for 30 to 40 minutes or until toothpick inserted in center comes out clean.

WHITE CHOCOLATE MACADAMIA BREAD

4 egg whites
Dash salt
½ cup sugar
½ cup flour
¾ cup macadamia nuts, roasted
¾ cup white chocolate chips

Preheat oven to 350 degrees. Grease a 5x9-inch loaf pan and line with parchment paper. Whip egg whites with salt until soft peaks form. Slowly add sugar and whip until sugar is dissolved and mixture is glossy and smooth. Fold in flour carefully; then fold in nuts and white chocolate chips just until combined. Spoon mixture into pan and bake for 50 minutes or until golden brown. Remove from oven and let cool. Preheat oven to 250 degrees and cut bread into thin slices with bread knife. Place slices in single layer on cookie sheet lined with parchment paper. Bake slices for 50 minutes or until completely dried out. Let cool for 20 minutes and store in airtight container.

NOT CHOCOLATY ENOUGH?

Dust your baking pan with cocoa powder instead of flour for an added touch of sweetness.

Quick
Tip

PULL-APART BREAD

4 tubes refrigerated biscuits
1½ cups sugar, divided
2 teaspoons cinnamon
⅓ cup brown sugar
1 cup butter
¼ cup semisweet chocolate chips

. . . .

Preheat oven to 350 degrees. Cut biscuits into quarters. Combine ¾ cup sugar with cinnamon. Roll each piece of biscuit in cinnamon-sugar mixture. Drop in greased Bundt pan. In saucepan, slowly bring remaining ¾ cup sugar, brown sugar, butter, and chocolate chips to a boil. Remove from heat. Pour over biscuits in pan. Bake for 30 to 45 minutes. Invert pan onto serving dish and serve immediately.

CHOCOLATE CINNAMON CHIP MUFFINS

2 cups biscuit baking mix
⅓ cup sugar
2 tablespoons vegetable oil
1 egg, slightly beaten
½ cup cinnamon chips
½ cup semisweet chocolate chips
⅔ cup milk

· ·

Preheat oven to 400 degrees. Line muffin pan with paper liners. In a large bowl, combine baking mix, sugar, vegetable oil, egg, cinnamon chips, chocolate chips, and milk. Fill muffin cups ⅔ full. Bake 15 to 18 minutes or until golden brown.

CHOCOLATE KISS BREAD

½ cup sugar
½ teaspoon cinnamon
20 milk chocolate kisses, unwrapped
2 tubes refrigerated biscuits
¼ cup butter, melted

Preheat oven to 350 degrees. Mix sugar and cinnamon. Press a chocolate kiss into each biscuit and close the dough around each kiss. Tip: Roll the biscuit around in the palm of your hand to help create a seal. Dip into melted butter and then roll in cinnamon mixture. Layer in a greased Bundt pan. Bake for about 25 minutes, until nicely browned. Let cool, as the chocolate centers will be hot.

MOCHA NUT BREAD

2 cups flour
1 cup sugar
1/3 cup cocoa
2 tablespoons instant coffee granules
1 teaspoon baking soda
2 eggs
1 1/4 cups sour cream
1/3 cup butter, melted
1 1/2 cups semisweet chocolate chips
1/2 cup chopped pecans

....

Preheat oven to 350 degrees. Grease 5x9-inch loaf pan. In large bowl, combine flour, sugar, cocoa, coffee granules, and baking soda. In another bowl, beat eggs, sour cream, and butter until smooth. Stir into dry ingredients just until moistened. Fold in chocolate chips and pecans. Pour into prepared pan. Bake for 55 to 60 minutes or until toothpick inserted in center comes out clean. Cool for 10 minutes before removing from pan to wire rack.

GERMAN CHOCOLATE BREAD

2 boxes German chocolate cake mix
2 small boxes instant chocolate pudding mix
1 (12 ounce) container sour cream
10 eggs
1½ cups oil
½ cup water
1 (12 ounce) package semisweet chocolate chips
1 cup flaked coconut

Preheat oven to 325 degrees. Mix together all ingredients. Pour into 3 greased loaf pans. Bake for 1 hour or until toothpick inserted in center comes out clean.

ORANGE CHOCOLATE MORSEL BREAD

1 ¼ cups orange juice from fresh-squeezed
   oranges
2 ½ teaspoons active dry yeast
4 cups flour
¼ cup sugar
1 tablespoon butter, softened
1 large egg
1 teaspoon orange extract
1 cup semisweet chocolate chips

Preheat oven to 350 degrees. Grease 5x9-inch
loaf pan. Heat orange juice until warm and add
yeast. Allow yeast to dissolve. In bowl, combine
flour, sugar, butter, egg, and orange extract. Stir in
yeast mixture and knead to form soft dough. Add
chocolate chips. Place in greased bowl, turning
once to coat. Cover and allow to rise until
doubled, about 1 ½ hours. Punch down; form in
prepared loaf pan and allow to rise again for about
1 hour. Bake for 20 to 25 minutes or until top is
browned.

CHOCOLATE CHIP BANANA MUFFINS

1 cup margarine
1 ¼ cups sugar
1 egg
3 ripe bananas
1 tablespoon instant coffee granules, dissolved in
  1 tablespoon water
1 teaspoon vanilla extract
2 ¼ cups flour
¼ teaspoon salt
1 teaspoon baking powder
1 teaspoon baking soda
1 cup semisweet chocolate chips

Preheat oven to 350 degrees. Blend together
margarine, sugar, egg, banana, coffee, and vanilla
in blender or food processor for 2 minutes. Add
flour, salt, baking powder, and baking soda. Blend
just until flour disappears. Add chocolate chips and
mix in with a wooden spoon. Spoon mixture into
18 paper-lined muffin cups. Bake for 25 minutes.

OATMEAL CHOCOLATE CHIP MUFFINS

1 ¼ cups quick-cooking oats
1 ¼ cups milk
1 egg
½ cup vegetable oil
¾ cup brown sugar, packed and divided
¾ cup semisweet chocolate chips
1 cup pecans, chopped and divided
1 ¼ cups flour
4 teaspoons baking powder
1 teaspoon salt

. . . .

Preheat oven to 400 degrees. In a medium bowl, combine oats and milk. Allow to stand for 15 minutes. Grease or line a muffin pan with paper liners. Stir egg, oil, ½ cup brown sugar, chocolate chips, and ½ cup pecans into the oat and milk mixture. In a large bowl, combine flour, baking powder, and salt. Add oat mixture to the flour mixture, stirring until just moist. Fill each muffin cup ⅔ full. Sprinkle tops with remaining brown sugar and pecans. Bake for 20 to 25 minutes.

SWAPPING CHOCOLATES

If you prefer to bake with an intense variety of dark chocolate (60% to 70% pure cocoa) instead of a milk chocolate or semisweet variety, you should use 25% to 35% less chocolate than your recipe calls for and add 1½ teaspoons more granulated sugar for each ounce of chocolate than the original recipe recommends.

Quick Tip

RASPBERRY WHITE CHOCOLATE MUFFINS

1 cup milk
½ and ¼ cup butter, melted and divided
1 egg, slightly beaten
2 cups flour
⅓ and ¼ cup sugar, divided
1 tablespoon baking powder
1 teaspoon salt
1 cup fresh or frozen raspberries
½ cup white chocolate chips

Preheat oven to 400 degrees. Line a muffin pan with paper liners. In a large bowl, combine milk, ½ cup butter, and egg. Stir in flour, ⅓ cup sugar, baking powder, and salt; stir just until flour is moistened. Gently stir in raspberries and white chocolate chips. Spoon batter into prepared baking cups. Bake for 24 to 28 minutes or until golden brown. Allow to cool slightly before removing from pan. Dip top of each muffin in remaining melted butter, then in remaining sugar.

CREAM CHEESE BISCUITS AND CHOCOLATE GRAVY

Biscuits:
- 2 cups biscuit baking mix
- 4 ounces cream cheese
- 1 tablespoon milk

Gravy:
- ⅓ cup sugar
- 1½ tablespoons flour
- 1½ tablespoons cocoa powder
- ½ cup milk
- ½ cup water
- ¼ cup butter
- 1 teaspoon vanilla extract

. . . .

Biscuits: Combine biscuit mix and cream cheese. Add milk to moisten the dough. Place dough on lightly floured surface and knead for 30 seconds. Roll out dough to desired thickness. Cut into rounds and place on greased baking sheet. Bake for 12 minutes or until browned.

Gravy: In small saucepan, whisk together sugar, flour, cocoa, milk, and water. Bring mixture to boil over medium heat, whisking constantly. Continue to boil until mixture thickens. Stir in butter and vanilla extract. Mix well and ladle over warm biscuits.

SIMPLE CHOCOLATE CROISSANTS

1 tube refrigerated crescent rolls
Mini chocolate chips
3 tablespoons melted butter
1 egg white
Powdered sugar
Sliced almonds

....

Preheat oven to 375 degrees. Unroll and separate crescent roll dough into triangles. Brush with melted butter. Sprinkle 1 to 2 teaspoons mini chocolate chips onto each triangle. Roll each triangle into crescent shape and place on ungreased cookie sheet. In small bowl, add 2 teaspoons water to egg white and mix well with fork or whisk. Brush the top of each croissant with egg wash. Top with sliced almonds, if desired. Bake for approximately 15 minutes. Let cool briefly and then remove from cookie sheet. Use a sieve to add a dusting of powdered sugar on top of each.

CINNAMON, CRANBERRY & CHOCOLATE BISCUITS

1¼ cups flour
1½ teaspoons cinnamon
⅔ cup brown sugar
⅔ cup cranberries
8 ounces chocolate, roughly chopped
¾ cup cooked quinoa, well drained
1 apple, grated
¼ cup vegetable oil

Preheat oven to 350 degrees. Sift flour and cinnamon into large bowl. Mix in brown sugar, cranberries, chocolate, and quinoa. In separate bowl, mix together the grated apple and the oil. Add apple mixture to dry ingredients and mix to combine. Place spoonfuls of the mixture onto greased baking sheet and bake for 30 minutes.

CHOCOLATE BREAKFAST BARS

1 ½ cups honey
4 tablespoons butter
2 ounces white chocolate
1 tablespoon vanilla
1 cup sunflower seeds
½ cup wheat germ or shredded coconut
⅔ cups crunchy peanut butter
1 cup dried fruit (like blueberries or strawberries)
5 cups quick oats

....

Boil honey, butter, and chocolate for 1 minute.
Remove from heat and add vanilla. Mix together
remaining ingredients and stir into the chocolate
mixture. Pour the dough onto a cookie sheet and
flatten it into one large rectangle about 1 inch
thick. Let cool, then cut into bars.

HAWAIIAN CHOCOLATE MUFFINS

⅓ cup vegetable oil
2 eggs
1 (8½ ounce) can crushed pineapple with juice
1¾ cups flour
¼ cup cocoa
⅓ cup sugar
3 teaspoons baking powder
½ cup macadamia nuts

....

Preheat oven to 400 degrees. Grease bottoms
only of 12 medium muffin cups or line with paper
baking cups. Beat oil, eggs, and pineapple together
in a large bowl. Stir in remaining ingredients just
until flour is moistened. Divide batter evenly
among muffin cups. Bake 20 to 25 minutes or until
a toothpick comes out clean. Remove muffins
from pan while still warm to minimize sticking.

CHOCOLATE SANDWICH FRENCH TOAST

3 eggs
1 cup milk
1 teaspoon sugar
1 teaspoon vanilla extract
$\frac{1}{4}$ teaspoon salt
12 slices day-old bread
3 milk chocolate candy bars, halved
2 tablespoons butter or margarine
Powdered sugar

....

Beat together eggs, milk, sugar, vanilla, and salt.
Pour half into ungreased 13x9-inch baking
dish. Arrange six slices of bread in a single layer
over egg mixture. Place one piece of chocolate
in the center of each piece of bread. Top with
remaining bread; pour remaining egg mixture
over all. Let stand for 5 minutes. In a large
nonstick skillet, melt butter over medium heat.
Fry sandwiches until golden brown on both
sides. Dust with powdered sugar. Cut sandwiches
diagonally; serve warm.

CHOCOLATE BANANA CREAM PANCAKES

2 cups vanilla pudding
2 cups cream cheese, softened
3 cups pancake mix, prepared
½ cup chocolate chips
1 banana, sliced
Chocolate sauce
1 tablespoon powdered sugar
Whipped topping

Blend vanilla pudding and cream cheese until smooth. Refrigerate immediately. Mix pancake batter according to package directions and preheat griddle over medium heat. Pour batter for two pancakes. Distribute chocolate chips and four banana slices per pancake onto batter in pan. Cook pancakes until golden brown on both sides. Allow pancakes to cool, then place first pancake upside down on a plate. Top with vanilla cream cheese mixture. Place second pancake upside down on top of the vanilla cream cheese mixture. Drizzle with chocolate sauce, sprinkle with powdered sugar, and garnish with whipped topping.

HAVE A GUILT-FREE BREAKFAST

Feeling guilty about indulging in chocolate for breakfast? Eating chocolate, particularly dark chocolate, actually has a lot of health benefits. It has up to eight times more antioxidants than strawberries and can lower cholesterol and blood pressure when consumed in small amounts on a daily basis. It also contains serotonin— a natural antidepressant.

Quick Tip

CHOCOLATE GRANOLA CRUNCH

3 cups regular oats
1 cup Cheerios
½ cup brown sugar
⅓ cup slivered almonds
½ teaspoon salt
¼ teaspoon cinnamon
¼ cup honey
2 tablespoons canola oil
1 teaspoon vanilla extract
2 ounces bittersweet chocolate, finely chopped
½ cup dried cranberries

Preheat oven to 300 degrees. In a large bowl, toss together oats, Cheerios, brown sugar, slivered almonds, salt, and cinnamon. In small saucepan, stir together honey and canola oil. Cook until warm over low heat (about 2 minutes). Remove from heat; stir in vanilla and chocolate until smooth. Drizzle over oat mixture. Coat hands lightly with nonstick cooking spray and gently mix chocolate mixture and oat mixture until combined. Scoop out mixture onto large baking sheet lined with parchment paper and spread evenly. Bake for 20 to 30 minutes, stirring every 10 minutes. Stir in cranberries once granola is baked. Place on wire rack until granola has cooled completely.

Decadent Drinks

*If any man thirst, let him come
unto me, and drink.*
JOHN 7:37

HOT CHOCOLATE

1 cup water
2 squares unsweetened chocolate
½ cup sugar
3 cups milk
1 teaspoon vanilla

In medium saucepan over low heat, cook water and chocolate until chocolate is completely melted and mixture is well blended, stirring constantly with whisk. Add sugar; mix well. Bring to a boil over medium-high heat. Boil for 3 minutes, stirring constantly. Gradually add milk, stirring with whisk until well blended. Stir in vanilla. Reduce heat to medium. Cook until mixture is heated through, stirring occasionally.

WHITE CHOCOLATE HOT COCOA

3 cups half-and-half, divided
¾ cup white chocolate chips
3 cinnamon sticks
⅛ teaspoon nutmeg
1 teaspoon vanilla
¼ teaspoon almond extract
Cinnamon

In medium saucepan, combine ¼ cup half-and-half, white chocolate chips, cinnamon sticks, and nutmeg. Whisk over low heat until chocolate is melted. Remove cinnamon sticks. Add remaining half-and-half. Whisk until heated through. Remove from heat. Stir in vanilla and almond extract. Serve warm in cups or mugs. Sprinkle with cinnamon.

CHOCOLATE HAZELNUT COFFEE

¾ cup hot water
¼ cup hot milk
2 teaspoons hazelnut-flavored instant coffee
   granules
1 teaspoon cocoa
1 tablespoon dark brown sugar
1 tablespoon whipped topping

Stir together all ingredients. Pour into mugs. Top
with whipped topping and serve immediately.

120

CHOCOLATE CHAI

1 bag black tea
½ cup boiling water
3 tablespoons sugar
2 tablespoons cocoa
2 cups milk
1 teaspoon vanilla
½ teaspoon nutmeg
Whipped topping

. . . .

In small saucepan, pour boiling water over tea bag. Cover and let stand for 3 to 5 minutes. Remove tea bag. Stir in sugar and cocoa. Cook and stir over medium heat just until mixture comes to a boil. Stir in milk, vanilla, and nutmeg; heat thoroughly. Do not boil. Pour into cups. Top with whipped topping.

$\frac{1}{3}$ cup white chocolate chips
2 cups half-and-half
2 cups hot fresh-brewed coffee
Whipped topping

In medium microwavable bowl, microwave chocolate chips and half-and-half on high for 2 minutes, stirring halfway through cooking time. Stir until chocolate is completely melted and mixture is smooth. Stir in coffee. Pour into large cups or mugs. Top each serving with whipped topping. Serve immediately.

STEAMING MOCHA COCOA

2 cups milk
2 teaspoons cocoa
2 tablespoons brown sugar
1 tablespoon ground coffee
1 teaspoon vanilla

Heat all ingredients in small saucepan and whisk until steaming. Strain and pour into 2 mugs.

MOCHA SPICED COFFEE

1½ teaspoons cinnamon
½ teaspoon nutmeg
5 cups fresh-brewed coffee
1 cup milk
¼ cup packed brown sugar
⅓ cup chocolate syrup
1 teaspoon vanilla

Mix cinnamon and nutmeg in with coffee grounds to make 5 cups coffee. Make coffee in coffeemaker. In heavy saucepan, combine milk, brown sugar, and chocolate syrup. Cook over low heat, stirring frequently and making sure milk does not boil. Once sugar is dissolved, add vanilla and brewed coffee.

* 1 ounce semisweet baking chocolate =
1 ounce unsweetened baking chocolate
plus 1 tablespoon sugar

* 1 cup semisweet chocolate chips =
6 ounces semisweet baking chocolate,
chopped

* 1 ounce unsweetened baking chocolate =
3 tablespoons baking cocoa plus 1
tablespoon vegetable oil or melted
shortening or margarine

DECADENT DRINKS

Quick
Chart

DECADENT DRINKS

1 cup hot water
¾ cup milk
2 tablespoons chocolate syrup
3 tablespoons caramel syrup
1 tablespoon instant coffee granules

Place all ingredients in microwave-safe bowl and microwave on high for 3 minutes or until hot. Stir and pour into mugs. Serve immediately.

PEPPERMINT TWIST WHITE HOT CHOCOLATE

4 cups milk
3 ounces white chocolate, chopped
⅓ cup red-and-white-striped candy canes or hard
    peppermint candies, crushed
⅛ teaspoon salt
Whipped topping
Additional red-and-white-striped candy canes,
    crushed

Bring milk to a simmer in saucepan. Reduce heat
to medium-low. Add white chocolate, crushed
candy, and salt; whisk until smooth. Ladle into
mugs, dividing equally. Serve with whipped topping
and additional crushed candy.

127

CHOCOLATE BANANA FIZZ

1 cup fat-free frozen vanilla yogurt
$\frac{1}{8}$ cup fat-free hot fudge syrup
1 banana, sliced
$\frac{1}{2}$ cup club soda

Place all ingredients in blender. Cover and blend on high speed until smooth. Serve immediately.

TWIST OF ORANGE HOT CHOCOLATE

2 cups milk
3 (1x2-inch) orange peel strips (orange part only)
$1/8$ teaspoon ground cinnamon
$1/2$ teaspoon instant espresso powder
4 ounces semisweet chocolate, grated

Combine all ingredients in saucepan. Stir over low heat until chocolate melts. Increase heat and bring to a boil, stirring often. Immediately remove from heat and whisk until frothy. Return to heat and bring just to a boil again. Repeat heating and whisking once again. Discard orange peel. Pour hot chocolate into two mugs.

1 cup milk
1 envelope instant hot chocolate mix
2 tablespoons butter
2 ounces milk chocolate, chopped
2 ounces bittersweet chocolate, chopped
6 ice cubes

. . . .

Heat milk in saucepan over medium-low heat until bubbles just begin to form around edges and mixture is heated through (approximately 2 minutes). Remove from heat; whisk in hot chocolate mix until well blended. Add butter, milk chocolate, and bittersweet chocolate; stir until smooth. Pour chocolate mixture into blender; add ice. Cover; blend on high speed until well blended. Serve immediately.

MALTED MILK BALL CHILLER

⅓ cup malted milk balls, crushed
1 cup ice cream
1½ tablespoons chocolate syrup
½ cup milk

Place all ingredients in blender and mix until creamy. Serve immediately.

MINTY CHOCOLATE MILK

2 tablespoons chocolate syrup
1/8 teaspoon peppermint extract
1 cup milk
1 scoop chocolate ice cream

Stir together chocolate syrup, peppermint
flavoring, and milk. Add ice cream. Serve
immediately.

CHOCOLATE CARAMEL PECAN SMOOTHIE

1 pint frozen chocolate yogurt
⅓ cup caramel ice cream topping
2 tablespoons chopped pecans
¾ cup milk

....

Place all ingredients in blender. Cover and blend on medium speed for 30 to 40 seconds or until smooth. Pour into 2 serving glasses.

Give your next cup of cocoa a flavorful
twist by stirring it with a candy cane,
cinnamon stick, or vanilla bean.

Quick
Tip

DECADENT DRINKS

CHOCOLATE PUNCH

¾ cup semisweet chocolate chips
2 cups hot water
½ cup sugar
2 quarts milk
2 teaspoons vanilla
1 quart club soda
1 quart vanilla ice cream

In small saucepan, melt chocolate chips over low heat. In large saucepan, add melted chocolate to water along with sugar. Heat chocolate mixture until just boiling, stirring constantly. Add milk and vanilla and cook until heated through. Combine with club soda in punch bowl and serve with scoops of ice cream.

FUDGY CHOCOLATE PUDDING SHAKE

1 cup milk
2 scoops ice cream
1 chocolate fudge brownie
2 tablespoons instant chocolate pudding mix
Whipped cream
1 ounce chocolate flakes

Combine milk, ice cream, brownie, and pudding powder in blender for 30 seconds. Let froth settle before pouring into glass. Add whipped cream and flaked chocolate.

136

MAYAN HOT CHOCOLATE

4 cups milk
½ cup unsweetened cocoa powder
1 teaspoon flour
¼ cup brown sugar
3 cloves, crushed
¼ teaspoon nutmeg
1 cinnamon stick (broken into pieces)
¼ teaspoon dried, crushed chili peppers
2 teaspoons powdered sugar
1½ teaspoon vanilla extract

Heat milk in double boiler over medium-low heat. Sift cocoa powder and flour together in a bowl. Add enough hot milk until a paste is formed. Add brown sugar, cloves, nutmeg, cinnamon stick, and chili peppers to the paste and stir the entire mixture into the remaining hot milk in the double boiler. Skim cloves and cinnamon stick pieces off the top with a slotted spoon. Add vanilla extract and powdered sugar. Serve hot.

CHOCOLATE EGGNOG

¾ cup heavy cream
1 ¼ cups grated bittersweet chocolate
2 cups milk
4 egg yolks
½ teaspoon vanilla extract
½ cup sugar
½ teaspoon nutmeg
¼ teaspoon allspice

Heat cream in saucepan over low heat until it just starts to boil. Place chocolate in a medium mixing bowl and pour hot cream over it. Reserve. Pour milk into saucepan and return to low heat. While milk heats, beat together remaining ingredients thoroughly. When milk begins to steam, shut off heat. Ladle one scoop of the hot milk into egg mixture. Whisk remaining milk, and slowly pour the egg/milk mixture into the rest of the milk. Whisk continuously on low heat for 20 minutes until mixture coats the back of a spoon. Pour over chocolate/cream mixture, stir together well, and chill thoroughly.

PUMPKIN HOT COCOA

1½ cups milk
2 tablespoons sugar
¼ teaspoon vanilla
½ square unsweetened chocolate
¼ cup canned pumpkin pie filling

Heat milk over low heat until it begins to steam. Add sugar, vanilla, and chocolate. Stir until well blended. Pour into mug and add pumpkin. Stir until well blended.

CHOCOLATE MINT TEA

¾ cup mint flavored tea
2 tablespoons chocolate syrup
¼ cup whipped topping
1 teaspoon sweetened chocolate powder

....

Prepare tea. Pour ¾ cup into mug and stir in
chocolate syrup. Top with whipped cream and
sprinkle with chocolate powder.

COOKIES & CREAM SHAKE

2 cups vanilla ice cream
I cup milk
8 cream-filled chocolate sandwich cookies
2 to 3 tablespoons instant coffee granules

Place ice cream, milk, cookies, and coffee granules in blender, and blend until smooth. Serve immediately.

ICED CHOCOLATE COLA FLOAT

2 ounces unsweetened chocolate
1/4 cup sugar
1 cup coffee or 1/2 cup espresso
2 1/2 cups hot milk
1 1/2 cups cola, chilled
Vanilla ice cream

Melt chocolate in double boiler. Stir in sugar.
Gradually stir in hot coffee or espresso, mixing
thoroughly. Add the milk and continue cooking
10 minutes until mixture is smooth, then cover
and chill. When ready to serve, stir in chilled cola.
Serve in a tall glass with a scoop of vanilla ice
cream.

NO MORE BURNT TONGUES

Need a cool way to chill your hot chocolate fast? Try freezing chocolate milk in an ice cube tray and dropping a few cubes into your mug. You'll be able to take that first delicious sip in no time.

(Quick Tip)

CHOCOLATE-MAPLE MALT FOR TWO

1 cup chocolate milk
1 cup vanilla ice cream
2 teaspoons instant malted milk powder
2 to 3 drops maple flavoring

Combine all ingredients in blender. Blend until smooth. Pour into glasses; serve immediately.